Mmmazing Mocktails: Refreshing Cocktail Recipes without the Alcohol

All rights Reserved. No part of this publication or the information in it may be quoted from or reproduced in any form by means such as printing, scanning, photocopying or otherwise without prior written permission of the copyright holder.

Disclaimer and Terms of Use: Effort has been made to ensure that the information in this book is accurate and complete, however, the author and the publisher do not warrant the accuracy of the information, text and graphics contained within the book due to the rapidly changing nature of science, research, known and unknown facts and internet. The Author and the publisher do not hold any responsibility for errors, omissions or contrary interpretation of the subject matter herein. This book is presented solely for motivational and informational purposes only.

Table of Contents

Mock Celebrity Champagne 5

Materniti 6

Baby Bump Breeze 7

Pre-Labor Love juice 8

Meno-Martini (for hot flashes) 9

Ginger Soda Mock tail 10

Margarita for Mommas 11

Pomegranate Spritzer 12

Mock-Punch 13

Slush Punch 14

Shiska Pomegranate Mock tail 15

Fake-tini 16

Cranberry Punch 17

Cider Punch 18

Berry Spritzer 19

Cucumber Lemonade 20

Hot Buttered Cider 21

Virgin Bellini's 22

Love Potion Non alcoholic 23

Pina Colada Float 24

Apple Spritzer 25

Mock Celebrity Champagne

Ingredients:
- 2 2 liter ginger Ale
- 2 can pineapple juice
- 1 bottle white grape juice

Directions:

I. Using a ring shaped cake pan add ½ ginger ale
II. Freeze and add more ginger ale to frozen ale
III. Place ring in serving bowl
IV. Add rest of ingredients to serving bowl
V. Serve

Materniti

Ingredients:
- 1 ½ oz. raspberry sorbet
- 4 oz. fresh orange juice
- Lime- pinch

Directions:

I.   Add everything into martini glass and enjoy

Baby Bump Breeze

Ingredients:
  I. 2 oz. chilled peach juice
  II. 2 oz. Sparkling wine
  III. Peach sliced to garnish

Directions:

  I. Add everything into glass and serve

Pre-Labor Love juice

Ingredients:
- 3 oz. cranberry juice
- Pineapple juice
- 7Up soda (pinch)

Directions:

I. Add everything to a shaker and enjoy a great drink without the alcohol.

Meno-Martini (for hot flashes)

Ingredients:
- ½ oz. raspberries
- ½ oz. lemon juice
- 1 oz. pineapple juice
- Ice

Directions:

I. Add ingredients to martini shaker and pour into sugar rimmed glass
II. Add lime to garnish

Ginger Soda Mock tail

Ingredients:
- Ginger root
- Sprite
- Lime

Directions:

I. Marinade the root in water for a few hours, then strain
II. Add to martini glass and add in sprite
III. Garnish with lime

Margarita for Mommas

Ingredients:
- 2 C sugar
- 3 C water
- Ice
- Mango, pitted
- 3 oz. mango syrup
- 1 ½ oz. lime juice

Directions:

I. Add everything and blend
II. Serve

Pomegranate Spritzer

Ingredients:
- 1-2 T pomegranate Juice
- 2 tsp sugar
- Oz. sparkling water

Directions:

I. Add the juice, sugar and waiter into glasses with ice
II. Serve

Mock-Punch

Ingredients:
- Can Pina colada
- 1 can froze orange pineapple juice
- 2 2liters, Diet Lemon lime soda
- 8 oz. crushed ice

Directions:

I. Add everything to your punch bowl
II. Maintain crushed ice to keep from watering down

Slush Punch

Ingredients:
- 6 C water
- 4 bananas
- 1 ½ C sugar
- 6 C pineapple juice
- 2 ½ oz. orange juice concentrate
- 1 ½ oz. pink lemonade
- 1 2 liters Sprite

Directions:

I. Blend 3 C water, bananas, and sugar until smooth and set aside
Add everything else into a saucepan and mix than add to blender, then add banana
II. Divide into small bags then freeze
III. When ready to serve pour into serving glasses

Shiska Pomegranate Mock tail

Ingredients:
- 2 C pomegranate Juice
- 2 C ice
- 2 T lime juice
- 1 T coconut water
- Stevia to taste

Directions:

I. Add everything into your food processor or a blender, and blend until liquid or desired consistency
II. Serve

Fake-tini

- 2 T cinnamon syrup
- 1 C apple cider
- Ice
- Cinnamon singer
- Apple slice to garnish

Directions:

I. Mix everything from first set of ingredients over medium heat, until sugar dissolved. Let cool and strain
II. Prepare martini glass, rim with the cinnamon sugar
III. Prepare your shaker with ice and cider with syrup
IV. Shake and pour

Cranberry Punch

Ingredients:
- 2 Qts. Cranberry juice
- 1 can pink lemonade (frozen but thawed)
- 1 Qt. sparkling water

Directions:

I. Add everything in a container and stir well

Cider Punch

Ingredients:
- 2 Qts. Apple cider
- 1 C sugar
- 1 tsp cinnamon
- 1 tsp. allspice
- 1 can orange juice concentrate
- 1 qt. chilled ginger

Directions:

I. Add your ingredients in saucepan and boil, until everything is sugar dissolves
II. Set in fridge until cold, and ready to serve

Berry Spritzer

Ingredients:
- 1 12-16 oz. Cranberry juice
- 1 2 liter of lemon lime (Sprite) soda

Directions:

I. Mix the two drinks and serve in cold pitcher
II. Serve

Cucumber Lemonade

Ingredients:
- 1 C sugar
- 1 T zest
- 1 C water
- ¼ C fresh mint
- 1 C lime juice
- 2 cucumber, thinly sliced
- 2 C sparkling water, chilled

Directions:

I. Add sugar, zest and water and boil until sugar is dissolves,
II. Remove from heat and add few drops of mint drops
III. Let sit for around 15-25 minutes
IV. Strain leaves, then and stir well, slowly
V. Let chill in fridge
VI. Serve after one hour

Hot Buttered Cider

Ingredients:
- ½ gallon apple cider
- ½ C lemon juice
- ½ C orange juice
- 1-2 cinnamon sticks
- 4 cloves
- 1 T butter

Directions:

I. Add ingredients over heat and simmer for 12-15 minutes, no boiling!
II. Serve with cinnamon sticks to garnish

Virgin Bellini's

Ingredients:
- 1 ½ C syrup recipe below
- 1 ¼ C pomegranate juice
- 1 C cranberry juice, cold
- 1 bottle sparkling water
- 2 limes

Syrup

- 1 C water
- 1 C sugar

Directions:

I. Make your syrup over the pan. You will take your water and sugar and boil, let sugar dissolve. Set aside until ready to serve
II. Blend drink ingredients together
III. Combine sauce and drinks

Love Potion Non alcoholic

Ingredients:
- 1 bottle club soda
- 4 oz. torani syrup
- 1/3 C ice, crushed
- Whipped cream

Directions:

I. Add everything in order as above and serve

Pina Colada Float

Ingredients:
- 3 T coconut milk
- 1 1/2 tsp Sugar
- 1/8 coconut extract
- ½ C sprite
- ½ C pineapple sherbet

Sherbet

- 1 ½ C buttermilk
- ½ C sugar
- 1/3 C yogurt
- 2 T light corn syrup
- 1 T heavy cream
- 3 C pineapple, puree

Directions:
I. Whisk first set of ingredients together, and add soda
II. Scoop pineapple into glass as well
III. Add your soda over the sherbet

Apple Spritzer

Ingredients:
- 2 T cranberry apple syrup
- Chilled Seltzer water
- Apple cider

Directions:

I. Add the syrup to your serving glass, to your desired taste
II. Top off with seltzer and cider
III. Garnish to taste

Printed in Great Britain
by Amazon.co.uk, Ltd.,
Marston Gate.